P9-BVH-491

SUGAR

A TRUE BOOK

by

Elaine Landau

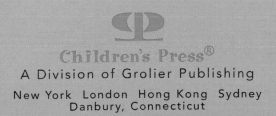

Children's Press®
A Division of Grolier Publishing
New York London Hong Kong Sydney
Danbury, Connecticut

A sugary treat

Reading Consultant
Linda Cornwell
*Coordinator of School Quality
and Professional
Improvement, Indiana State
Teachers Association*

Author's Dedication
To Joshua Gramizo

**Visit Children's Press® on the
Internet at:
http://publishing.grolier.com**

Library of Congress Cataloging-in-Publication Data

Landau, Elaine.
   Sugar / Elaine Landau.
      p.   cm. — (A true book)
   Includes bibliographical references and index.
   Summary: Examines the history, sources, refinement, and uses of sugar.
   ISBN 0-516-21027-0 (Lib. bdg.)   0-516-26772-8 (pbk.)
   1. Sugar—Juvenile literature. [1. Sugar.] I. Title. II. Series.
TP378.2.L36 1999
664'.1—dc21
                                    98-47334
                                        CIP
                                        AC

GROLIER
PUBLISHING

Contents

A party, or a trip to the ice cream shop, wouldn't be the same without sugar.

It's Everywhere

Sugar in the morning—
Sugar in the evening—
Sugar at suppertime—
These may be the words
to an old song, but there's
more to sugar than that.
Some people say sugar is
what makes life sweet. That's
a matter of opinion. But

without a doubt, sugar makes many foods tasty. It's what makes the icing on a birthday cake the best part, or a hot fudge sundae a treat to eat.

But sugar isn't just found in desserts. Did you ever eat a frosted toaster pastry for breakfast? There's sugar in it. There's also sugar in muffins, Danishes, and many of the jams and jellies that go on them. Have you enjoyed a

Sugar is a key ingredient in many baked goods and drinks.

cold soda or lemonade on a warm summer's day? There's sugar in these products as well.

Many sauces and condiments have a taste we like, thanks to sugar.

However, it may surprise you to know that sugar also exists in many other foods. Foods we don't usually think of as being especially sweet have sugar as an ingredient. These foods include salad dressings, tomato sauce, and hot dog relish.

Some nonfood products contain sugar. It is used both in tanning leather and in making some plastics. You may not always realize it, but sugar is a part of everyday life.

Sugar

Take a good look at the sugar in a sugar bowl. It's made up of small white grains called granules. Yet it didn't always look that way. It probably started off as part of either the sugarcane or sugar beet plant.

All green plants manufacture (make) sugar. This occurs

These granules began as either a stalk of grass or a root.

through a process called photosynthesis. During photo-synthesis, plants turn the sun's energy into food. However, the greatest amounts of this sugar (also known as sucrose) are produced in sugarcane and sugar beets. Therefore, these crops are grown for the sugar they supply.

Sugarcane is actually a giant grass. A fully grown field of sugarcane looks like a sea of tall grass. The stalk is

A sugarcane field in Hawaii

Varieties of sugarcane

divided into several jointed parts. It looks something like a stick of bamboo. Sugarcane plants also have long, narrow leaves. But the stalk contains the sweet juice from which sugar is made.

Sugarcane is a warm-weather plant. It's grown in tropical and subtropical places. Besides a hot, sunny climate, sugarcane also needs a good deal of rainfall. Most sugarcane in the United States is grown in Louisiana, Florida, and Hawaii.

The sugar beet is another major source of sugar. In the United States most sugar beets are grown in California, Idaho, Michigan, Minnesota,

Sugar beet plants

and North Dakota. Sugar
beets need cooler climates
than sugarcane.

You could never mistake a
sugar beet for sugarcane. The

sugar beet has a long, thick, fleshy white root topped with large green leaves. Its sugar is stored in its root. But even though sugarcane and sugar beets do not look at all alike, there is no difference in the sugar they provide.

There are other forms of sugar besides that of sugar-cane and sugar beets. These are some:

Maple Sugar—This sugar comes from the sap of sugar maple trees. American Indians

Maple tree sap is collected in buckets, then poured off and boiled down to maple syrup.

used this sweetener long before Europeans ever came to America.

Honey—Honey is actually a mixture of sugars. It is formed by bees from nectar. Nectar is the sweet fluid collected from some flowers by bees.

Cornstarch and Other Starches—Cornstarch is used to make corn syrup. Food manufacturers use corn syrup to sweeten soft drinks, canned fruits, jams, and other items.

A honey bee gathers nectar for honey.

All these sugars have been used as sweeteners at various times. However, our main sugar supply comes from sugarcane and sugar beets.

Sugar is an important product worldwide. The United States produces over 7.5 million tons of sugar annually (each year). But sugar isn't only produced in the United States. India produces more sugar than any other country in the world. Brazil, China, and France are also large sugar producers.

From Field to Table

When the sugarcane in a field has ripened, it's ready for harvesting. How the cane is picked depends on where it's grown. In some parts of the world, sugarcane is still cut and gathered by hand. But in the United States, machines known as

A worker harvests sugarcane in Cuba (top). Machine harvesting in Louisiana (bottom)

soldier or combine harvesters
are used.

Soldier harvesters first cut
off the cane tops. Next, the
stalks are cut and laid in heaps
behind the machine. You might
be surprised to learn that
these sugarcane heaps are
then burned for a few minutes.

Believe it or not, sugarcane farmers
have this blaze under control.

This is to remove any dried leaves or field debris (trash). The stalks aren't damaged by the fire. Their moisture and tough outer coating keep them from burning.

Afterward, cane loaders place the sugarcane in large transport wagons. The wagons bring it to either a raw-sugar factory or a transloader station. At a transloader station, the cane is transferred to a high-way trailer to be delivered to a factory at a distant location.

Trucks transport heaps of sugarcane to the factory.

If the sugar is picked with a combine harvester, things are done a bit differently. The stalks are cut into short pieces called billets. Extractor fans are used to blow away the leaf trash. Then the billets are taken to the factories.

The cane is washed soon after it arrives at the processing plant.

At a raw-sugar factory, the cane is weighed. It is also sampled to test for quality. The sugarcane is then washed and crushed. Its juice is boiled down to make a thick syrup. This syrup is separated into sugar crystals (raw sugar) and molasses. The molasses is used in livestock (farm animal) feed.

Once the sugar has been taken from the sugarcane, a woody material remains. This cane by-product is called bagasse. Bagasse is used as a

Stripped of their sugar, the cane stalks become bagasse, another useful product.

fuel in factories. But it can also be used in making paper, building boards, plastics, mulch, and animal bedding or litter.

The raw sugar, which is a yellowish brown color, is sold to a sugar refinery. At the refinery, the raw-sugar crystals are melted. Their color and any remaining impurities are removed. The sugar will leave the site as white or "refined" sugar.

Sugar is extracted (taken)
from the sugar beet plant a bit
differently. Following a harvest,
the beets are delivered to a

factory. Then they are washed
to remove any dirt from the
field. The clean beets are
sliced into thin pieces called
cosettes. These cosettes are
put in special machines
known as diffusers. Inside the
diffusers, the cosettes soak in

hot water. This helps release their sugary juice. The fluid obtained is processed into white or refined sugar. Like the sugarcane product, it could end up in your sugar bowl.

This warehouse stores tons of processed sugar.

Sweets for

Making candy and cookies is often the best part of holiday preparation. But these simple recipes will help make any day special. Be sure an adult supervises, and don't forget to have fun sharing the results!

Sugar Cookies

Wash your hands well, and preheat the oven to 350° F (175° C).

You will need:
1/2 cup of butter, softened
1/2 cup of margarine, softened
1 egg
1 teaspoon lemon or almond extract
2 cups of white sugar
2 1/2 cups of self-rising flour

Beat all the ingredients, except the flour, with an electric mixer until fluffy. Add the flour and mix well.

Roll the dough into balls, then flatten on an ungreased cookie sheet. Bake for 5 to 8 minutes until done. Makes about 4 1/2 dozen cookies.

the Sweet

Angel Food Candy

You will need:
1 cup of sugar
1 cup of dark corn syrup
1 tablespoon of vinegar
1 tablespoon of baking soda
1 pound of chocolate, melted

In a heavy saucepan, combine the sugar, corn syrup, and vinegar. Cook over medium heat, stirring constantly until the sugar dissolves. Then cook without stirring until the temperature reaches 300° F ("hard crack stage") on a candy thermometer. Do not overcook!

Remove the pan from the heat and quickly stir in the baking soda. Pour the mixture into a buttered oblong or rectangular pan. When cool, break into bite-size pieces. Dip these in the melted chocolate, then place on waxed paper until the chocolate is firm. Makes about 1 1/2 pounds.

A Sweet History

Through the years, people have looked for ways to sweeten their food. Honey was the earliest sweetener. Researchers think that ancient people may have even crushed certain flowers to drink their nectar (the sweet fluid within the flower).

Before sugarcane farming began, honey from the comb provided sweetness.

It's likely that sugarcane was grown in India even before 400 B.C. When the conqueror Alexander the Great and his armies swept through the region they found fields of this crop. The men had never seen anything like it before. They described it as a tall grass that produces a honeylike juice without the help of bees!

Raising sugarcane spread to China by about 100 B.C. Yet, for a long time sugar remained quite costly. It was considered a luxury reserved for royalty and the very rich.

Hundreds of years later, sugar was grown in the warmer areas of Europe. By then it had become more readily available to the public. In the 1400s, when European explorers or settlers headed for other parts of the world, they often brought sugarcane with them. The

Christopher Columbus planted sugarcane on the Caribbean islands in 1493 (above). An early 19th-century sugarcane processing plant (right).

Portuguese planted it in parts of Africa and Brazil.

In 1751, Jesuit priests brought sugarcane to Louisiana. They grew it near their church in New Orleans. A number of sugarcane plantations soon sprang up nearby. And in time sugarcane was grown in other warm regions of the United States.

Like sugarcane, the sugar beet was also grown in ancient times. People in Babylonia, Egypt, and Greece used its sugar to sweeten foods. In the 1800s, sugar beet mills were common in Europe and Russia.

Later on, sugar beets were successfully raised in the United States. The first sugar beet factory was established in Alvarado, California, in 1870.

Are Sweets Bad for You?

Sugar is a carbohydrate. Carbohydrates are a group of foods that provide the body with energy. In their natural state, sugarcane and sugar beets also contain important vitamins and minerals. However, these are mostly removed when the sugar is

Sugarcane stalks and juice are popular products at this roadside stand in Ecuador.

refined. Therefore, sugar's major value is as a source of energy.

However, sugar has often been blamed for a number of health and behavior problems. Some people claim that sugar can play a role in poor school performance. It has also been

The sugar we eat gives us energy for play, as well as for our studies at school.

said to worsen or even cause hyperactivity. Hyperactive children tend to be overly active, and have difficulty paying attention for long periods. Yet, a recent study shows that there may not be a connection between sugar and this condition.

It's also been said that sugar is addictive to children. This means that once their bodies become used to sugar—they will crave it. But medical researchers stress that this isn't true.

Of course, eating too much sugar can cause some problems. It can lead to tooth decay as well as to being overweight. But there's a place for some sugar within a balanced diet. After all, the human body can't tell the difference between the sugar in a peach and that from a sugar

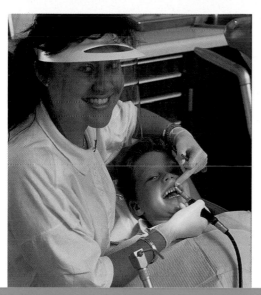

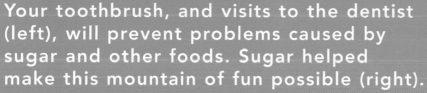

Your toothbrush, and visits to the dentist (left), will prevent problems caused by sugar and other foods. Sugar helped make this mountain of fun possible (right).

bowl. Unlike artificial sweeteners, a package of sugar contains no chemicals or warnings. And foods containing sugar may just be among the best-tasting ones we eat.

To Find Out More

Here are some additional resources to help you learn more about sugar:

Books

Burns, Diane L. **Sugaring Season: Making Maple Syrup.** Carolrhoda, 1990.

Gibbons, Gail. **The Honey Makers.** Morrow Junior Books, 1997.

London, Johnathan. **The Sugaring Off Party.** Dutton Children's Books, 1995.

Nottridge, Rhoda. **Sugars.** Carolrhoda, 1993.

Organizations and Online Sites

Cookie Recipe.com
http://cookierecipe.com

"Desperate for cookies?" This site features a different cookie recipe for every day of the year. Includes an International Cookie Glossary, ingredient conversion tables, and tips on mailing cookies.

Indiana Sugars
Suite 320
745 McClintock Drive
Burr Ridge, IL 60521
http://www.sugars.com

Provider of sugars, liquid sweeteners, baker's supplies, and more. Visit the Sweetener Resource Center to find out about beet refining, sugar nutrients and chemistry, and U.S. sugar growers.

The Sugar Association
1101 15th Street N.W.
Suite 600
Washington, D.C. 20005
http://www.sugar.org/

The scoop on sugar—how it's grown and processed, types of sugar, and information on the U.S. sugar industry. Click on the sugar packet marked "Kids" for tips on staying healthy.

Sugar Information
http://www.sugarinfo.co.uk/

The first and largest free international sugar industry guide.

U.S. Sugar Corporation
111 Ponce de Leon Avenue
Clewiston, FL 33440
http://www.ussugar.com/

The nation's largest producer of cane sugar, with a profile of how the industry affects the Everglades environment.

Important Words

bagasse the woody material that remains after the sugar is removed from sugarcane stalks

billets short pieces of the sugarcane's stalk

cosettes thin slices of the sugar beet plant used in making refined or white sugar

debris trash or rubbish

harvest to gather a crop

impurities unwanted materials, such as dirt particles

manufacture to make or produce in large quantities

photosynthesis the process through which plants use the sun's energy to make food

sap the fluid part of a plant

sucrose the sugar found in sugarcane and sugar beets; when refined, sucrose becomes white sugar

Index

Meet the Author

Elaine Landau worked as a newspaper reporter, an editor, and a youth services librarian before becoming a full-time writer. She has written more than one hundred nonfiction books for young people, including True Books on dinosaurs, animals, countries, and food.

Ms. Landau, who has a bachelor's degree in English and journalism from New York University and a master's degree in library and information science from Pratt Institute, lives in Florida with her husband and son.